"There is a reason that Isaiah tells us to ask ... ...
and stand in them. Nothing stimulates our faith faster than
being reminded of what God has already accomplished in,
through and for others. Kathie in her book takes us far into
the past and reminds us that God doesn't need flawless vessels
through which to reveal Himself, only willing ones. This book
is a must read for every believer, for those walking in faith and
those needing too. I recommend it highly."

----Iverna Tompkins,
Teacher

"Kathie Walters has an amazing ability in her writings to ignite
a fresh fire in your heart. The lives of the early Celtic
Christians she is telling us of, will encourage you to come to a
new level of intimacy with Jesus in your own personal
fellowship."

"The fire of the Lord was lit in Ireland through a bold and
godly group of men and women. They gave themselves whole
heartedly to prayer in order to bring the message of the gospel
with power to the people of Ireland, Scotland, England and
Wales."

"When they walked into villages and towns and declared the
Gospel message, signs, wonders and miracles accompanied
their ministry. Kings and rulers were won because of them
and the fires were lit through their lives."

----Suzanne Hinn

"The life of one of the world's greatest saints is only remembered as a kind of celebration of the Irish, but St. Patrick was a mighty man of prayer and power whose life changed the part of the world we call The British Isles. And because many of us are descendants of that area, our lives have been impacted by this great man of God."

"I am confident that the life of St. Patrick is relevant to us today. He lived in pagan times, and in a pagan land. The world we live in is fast regressing into the same type of paganism. By reading how St. Patrick fearlessly took his stand against all the hordes of hell, that laid claim to what they thought was their territory, we will learn how we too can overturn the kingdom of Satan through the power of God. I cannot emphasize enough how important it is to study the life of this mighty man of God and others of his day, from Brigid, Cuthbert, to Brendan, Kieran and the abbott of the famous monastery at Bangor, Comgall."

----Gwen Shaw,
Founder, End-Time Handmaidens and Servants

"Kathie Walters found a gold mine when she rediscovered the treasure of the Celtic Christians and their depth of spirituality. If you want to mine the depths of God—and go deeper in intimacy with Him—then the writings of these early Christians will help you reach that goal."

----J. Lee Grady,
Editor, Charisma

"Just as the scribes drew from their treasure, old and new, (Matt 13:52) there is a great value in learning from those who walked with God in the past. The signs and wonders of the early Celtic church will inspire us today, to press in and live in all that God has for us now."

----Joy Strang,
Strang Communications, Lake Mary, Florida

"The early Celtic pioneers of faith were people of "The Book" seeking to find purity of faith in their community and lives, and finding miracles in austerity and everyday life. They were drawn together in their quest by the regularity of their lives, especially in prayer and praise at regular and set times of the day and night."

"In reading the lives of the "Saints" the apparent disharmony of nature became a source of repose and strong faith in God's love; by faith they often took total control of the elements."

"In their travels, they always endeavored to reach the king or prince, knowing that if he came to faith in Christ thousands of his subjects would follow suit. Their great gift of hospitality is still a way of life for the people of Ireland."

----Jack A. Gamble
Emerald Isle Books
Belfast, N. Ireland

"The Lord was clear when He told His people (Deut 4:9..) "Only be careful, and watch yourselves closely so that you do not forget the things your eyes have seen or let them slip from your heart as long as you live. Teach them to your children and to their children after them." We are to be instructed and exhorted by what God did with our spiritual ancestors. Kathie Walters continues to seek out and recover a wealth of buried treasure in the history of some of these great men and women of God. I am sometimes embarrassed, after reading some of her works, at how little I know about the mighty Champions of God who have lived since the resurrection."

----Steve Shultz,
The Elijah List, www.elijahlist.com

"*Celtic Flames* will bless your socks off! The Father is calling us to deeper intimacy with Him. This can only transpire through those precious throne room experiences as the Celtic fathers had. This anointed book will challenge the reader to pursue this kind of intimate relationship with God. Kathie is a gifted prophetess and author."

----Dr. Paul N. Gervais,
Augusta, Maine

Celtic Flames

Kathie Walters

- Patrick
- Brendan
- Brigid
- Cuthbert
- Columba
- Kieran
- Comgall

Foreword by
Ruth Ward Heflin

Copyright © 1999 Kathie Walters
All rights reserved
Printed in the United States of America
ISBN: 1-888081-55-4

1st Printing December 1999

Published by
GOOD NEWS MINISTRIES
220 Sleepy Creek Road
Macon, Georgia 31210

Layout and Graphics by
Quality Computer Works
<><

saylor@hom.net

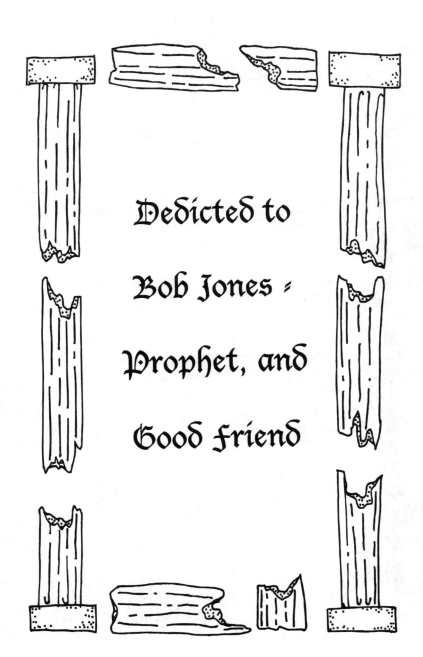

Dedicted to

Bob Jones –

Prophet, and

Good Friend

Foreword

Kathie Walters is being used of God in this hour to raise up the foundations of former generations as Isaiah prophesied. Her understanding of the 4th, 5th, and 6th century revivals challenge us to believe for kings, rulers, presidents, prime ministers and others in authority to know God.

Kathie shows us clearly that there were Elijah anointings and Mount Carmel successes in the early centuries that we need to walk in again as we come to the new Millennium. These apostles of old had great signs, wonders and miracles accompanying their prophetic words, which are clearly recorded in this book.

Reading her writing stirs up a simple faith for the demonstrations once again of Celtic Flames in our day.

Ruth Ward Heflin

Credits

Unless otherwise stated, all information is taken from the vast resources of Very Rev. John O'Hanlon- Member Royal Irish Academy.

Rev. O'Hanlon's *Lives of the Irish Saints*, (1875), consist of Rev John O'Hanlon's research into many hundreds of historic documents and papers. Many now contained in various museums, universities, and churches around the world.

Rev. John O'Hanlon was born in Stradbally, Queen's County April 30th 1821 and educated first in his native place and then at Ballyroan and again at Stradbally. He obtained a first class classical education. He Entered Carlow college in 1840 and stayed until May 1842.

Rev. O'Hanlon went to Quebec with relatives proceeding then to the United States. His experiences in the United States are told in his *Life and Scenery in Missouri*. Published over the signature of *An Irish Missionary Priest.*

He was ordained by Archbishop Kenrick in 1847 and returned to Ireland in 1853. He held various appointments in Dublin, and in 1885 was made Canon by Archbishop Walsh. In 1891 he went to the United States to assist in the golden jubilee of the Archbishop who had ordained him.

Canon O'Hanlon was one of those most eminent of Irish scholars and Hagiologists. He died May 15 1905.

He wrote history, poetry biography, topography. *His Lives of the Irish Saints* (9 volumes) appeared in a colossal work - a life-time task for any ordinary writer. He also wrote 2 volumes of *Irish American History*.

Many Thanks

To Jack Gamble at Emerald Isle Books, 539 Antrim Rd. Belfast BT15 3BU. N Ireland. For all of his efforts to find me some of the hidden treasures of the early Celtic church.

Other Books by Kathie Walters and Information on Kathie's Ministry:

Angels - Watching Over You
Living in the Supernatural
Spirit of False Judgment
The Visitation
Parenting - By the Spirit
Columba-the Celtic Dove

Available from Good News Ministries,
220 Sleepy Creek Road
Macon, Ga 31210

Phone (912) 757 8071
Fax   (912) 757 0136
e-mail goodnews@hom.net
www.goodnews.netministries.org

CONTENTS

CELTIC FLAMES

THE MIRACULOUS BIRTH AND DEATH OF THE CELTIC SAINTS

Looking at the many prophesies that have come forth in the last few years about the powerful anointing God wants to bring to the end time church, I found myself looking back to the early Celtic Christians, who had an awesome relationship with God. Certainly they were on a different faith level as far as the supernatural was concerned; what was normal to them seems beyond us today. Surely the end-time church should have as much power and revelation and relationship with God, if not more, than these 4th-5th-6th-century Christians. So let's take a look at their lives and deaths and consider their sacrifice and commitment. God hasn't changed. He is the same; His power has not diminished; it is still available.

Kathie Walters

BRENDAN OF CLONFERT
A.D. 448 - A.D. 581

BRENDAN'S BIRTH

Brendan's father, Findlug, who lived in Alltraighe Caile, a district in Ciaraige, Ireland, was married to a devout Christian woman and they were under the ministry of Bishop Erc. Brendan's mother had a vision of herself when she was pregnant, and in the vision, her bosom was full of gold. When she asked Bishop Erc the meaning of the vision, he told her that the baby she was carrying would be full of grace and full of the Holy Spirit.

On the night of Brendan's birth, the chief prophet of Ireland, Becc mac De, was visiting the house of a wealthy landowner, Airdi. Becc mac De began to prophesy that a worthy king (Brendan), would be born that night between Airdi's house and the ocean, and that he would take many kings and princes with him to heaven.

Bishop Erc also saw in the Spirit, Alltraighe Caile, in a great blaze and a multitude of angels shining in white, all around the land. Bishop Erc rose early the next morning and went to the house of Findlug. He took the child into his arms and prophesied, "O Man of God and destined servant of God, accept me as thy own monk (teacher), and though many are joyful at your birth, my heart and soul are even more joyful." Although the name "Mobi" had been given to the child, a drop of fair oil was seen upon his forehead so he was called "Brendan," which means Fair drop.

ITA

Brendan was taken to be fostered first by Ita, herself a famous Celtic nun, who loved him dearly. Ita often saw angels in attendance to Brendan during the five years he was with her.

BISHOP ERC

After his time with Ita, Brendan went to study with Bishop Erc. During that time Brendan asked for milk but there was none available. Erc however, said that he didn't see a problem with that request. Every day after that a doe came from Slieve Lougher with her fawn to give milk.

BRENDAN AND THE GIRL

One day when Brendan was young he accompanied Bishop Erc on a ministry trip to preach the Gospel. Bishop Erc left him in the chariot (wagon) alone for a while. A young girl, the king's daughter, came to the chariot, and seeing how pleasant he was to look at, she tried to play and flirt with him. Brendan asked her, "What brought you here? Be off home." With that he took the reigns in his hand and began to beat her, until she ran crying to her father.

Meanwhile, Bishop Erc returned and severely rebuked Brendan. For punishment he left him alone for the night in a cave, but unbeknown to Brendan, he stayed close by. Brendan began to sing praise to God and say Psalms aloud. His voice was heard a mile away and Bishop Erc saw angels coming and going between earth and heaven all night. It is said that the following day it was difficult to look upon the face of Brendan because his complexion was so bright.

BARINTHUS' TALE

Several years later, when Brendan came to a place called Leim na Subaltaige, he met a godly brother named Barinthus, grandson of King Niall. Barinthus told Brendan of an island he had once visited, called the Island of Promise. He said that God had promised the island to those who would come after him. Brendan was so affected by Barinthus' tale of the island that he took fourteen of his monks to pray and seek the Lord about it. After fasting and praying Brendan heard the voice of an angel speaking to him saying, "Arise, Brendan, for that which you have requested, you will receive of God, - that is, to visit the Island of Promise."

THE ANGEL

Brendan saw the island in a vision and shortly the angel came to him again and said, "From now on, I will ever be with you, and I will show you one day the fair island which you have seen by the Spirit, and which you desire to find." Brendan wept for joy and gave thanks to God.

After making three boats ready, sixty men left the coast with Brendan to seek the will of God. They visited many islands which God ordained for them and met many of God's people. As they arrived at the island of the Paradise of Birds to keep the Easter festival, they were met by the Procurator who greeted them joyfully. He brought them all kinds of food, and water to celebrate the festival.

THE PROPHECY THROUGH THE BIRD

When they sat down at the table to eat, a bird alighted on the prow of the ship and began to sing. Brendan perceived that the bird had been sent with a message for them, and the bird then prophesied, "The day of the Lord's supper you will spend with the Procurator. Every Easter you will spend on the same island, and from Easter to Pentecost with us and Christmas in the Isle of Ailbe. And at the end of the seventh year you will be borne to the land which you are seeking, and you will be there forty days. After that you shall be carried by the wind to your own land."

On hearing this, Brendan bowed himself to the ground and wept and gave thanks and praise to God. The bird then returned to its own place. Brendan left the island three days later and sailed for forty days and nights. The men with him became concerned that they would have nowhere to celebrate Easter but Brendan assured that God was able to supply a place, and he remembered the prophetic word given through the bird.

THE ISLAND OF THE HERMIT

They passed by several islands and eventually drew near to one of them. Brendan began to prophesy to his men about a man who was living on that island. "You shall shortly see a hermit of this island named Paul who has received sustenance from a special animal." When they found a suitable place to dock the boat, Brendan told them to stay until he obtained permission for them to come ashore. When Brendan came to the summit of the island, he saw two caves with a waterfall in front of them. As he stood before the caves, a very old man came toward him. "It is good for brethren to come together," he said and bade Brendan call the other men from the boat.

When they came the old man greeted them and kissed them and called them by their own name one by one. Brendan was so amazed at the man's countenance, which was glorious, and by his knowing their names, that he wept and sobbed, saying, "I am not worthy to wear the monk's habit."

Paul, the old servant of God, said to Brendan, "O honored father, very many are the miracles which have been revealed to you, and you say in your heart that you are not worthy to wear the habit of a monk, but I say unto you, you are more than any monk who is nourished by the labor of his own hands, for God has fed and clothed you supernaturally out of His own secret treasure."

Brendan asked Paul how he came to that island and where he was from previously. Paul answered, "I was brought up in the monastery of Patrick for fifty years. I was in charge of the cemetery of the brothers. My Abbot one day pointed to the sea and said, 'Tomorrow go there and you will find a boat which will bear you to a place where you will remain until the day of your death.' I did as he told me and for three days I rowed and then left off the oars and I let the boat drift for seven days and let it be led by the Lord. Thus I came to this island and here I have stayed, giving myself to prayer and intercession." Paul continued, "The first day an otter came and brought me a fish to eat. After that the otter came every third day and brought the same. The stream and waterfall brought water, and I have been here for 90 years, and fifty with Patrick. Now at 140 years I am still awaiting the day of my account."

PAUL'S PROPHECY TO BRENDAN

Paul prophesied to Brendan, "Get ready to depart and take some of the water from the fountain with you, for you have a journey of 40 days until Easter and then you will keep the festival as you have done for this last seven years. After that you will reach land which is exceeding holy, more than any other and you will remain there for 40 days. After that God will bring you in safety to your own native land."

Everything happened as Paul had prophesied. Brendan visited many islands on his journey and had many confrontations with demons, but also received many blessings from God.

THE ISLAND OF PROMISE

Eventually they found the place that was promised to Brendan, the Island of Promise. As they came near to the island, they heard a voice speaking. An old man who was on the island, said, "O much traveled men, holy pilgrims, you who look for heavenly rewards, laboring and looking for this land, rest a little from your labor now." When they had rested, the same elder said to them, "Do you realize that this lovely land has never seen blood spilt? Nor any sinner or evildoer has been buried here. Leave everything in the boat and come up here." When they came ashore, he greeted them and kissed each of them and wept with joy. "Search and see the border of this paradise," he said, "There is no sickness, there is pleasure without contention; union without quarrel, the attendance of angels, and meadows sweet with the scent of flowers. Happy indeed would you be Brendan, son of Findlug, to inhabit forever this island."

Brendan and his companions marveled and were astonished at the wonders of God. The elder spoke with a voice like that of an angel, "Let us all pray silently." After a while Brendan asked him, "Is it God's will that I stay here until I leave this earth?" The elder answered, "He who seeks his own will opposes the will of God. It is sixty years since I came here," he said, "And the food of angels has fed me all that time. Christ bade me wait here for you, and now you have come to me, it is time for me to go to heaven. And when you have departed for your own land, instruct the men of Erin, for crimes and sins shall be corrected by you."

After they partook of the Lord's supper and prayed together, the elder sent his spirit to God. The sailors buried his body with great reverence and honor.

IRELAND AND BRITAIN

After his time on the island, Brendan headed back to Ireland according to the prophecy. Sometime later he went to Britain and did many wonderful miracles. He built a monastery named Bleit in the district of Letha. One night Brendan had a vision which he spoke little of, it told of a great heresy with regard to the faith and made Brendan afraid. He left and returned to Ireland.

CLONFERT

Brendan built a monastery in Clonfert. This was just after the time of the famous battle fought about Columcille with Diarmait mac Cerbaill.

Brendan did many miracles, and raised the dead. He delivered the demonized and saved the souls of many men and women of Ireland, by the grace and power of God.

MUSIC

Brendan refused to listen to any music and when asked why, he replied that once Michael, the Archangel, had come from the Lord to play him music and there was none sweeter. When music was played in his presence, it is said that he would stuff his ears.

Holiness and a great zeal and passion for God were hallmarks of Brendan's ministry, as in many others, Columba, Patrick, Kiaran, Colman, Brigid, Maedoc of Ferns, Coemgen, Berach- to name a few.

BRENDAN PROPHESIES ABOUT HIS DEATH

At the end of Brendan's life he went to visit his sister, Brig, at the Fort of Aed (Annadown in County Galway). The record in *Irish Lives*, by O'Hanlon says, "He raised the dead, cleansed the lepers, gave sight to the blind and hearing to the deaf. He healed many sick people, cast out many devils, founded many churches and cells, appointed abbots and put down crimes." After many great, perilous voyages

Brendan drew near to the day of his death. He spoke to the brethren after the church service one Sunday, "God is calling me to His eternal kingdom; my body must be taken to Clonfert, for there will be the attendance of angels and there will be my resurrection." He instructed them to take a small chariot and allow only one person drive it, so as not to attract attention and cause people to dispute over his body. "A young man with only one eye, the left one, to speak precisely, will meet the bearer of my body, viz. Cuirrine, a son of Setna. And he will say to the brother bringing the body, 'Is that the body of Brendan that you have?' He will say in a rough voice, 'Among us shall be his resurrection, give up the body.'" Then said Brendan, "Let the brother offer Cuirrine a mass of gold to allow him continue to Clonfert."

Brendan continued to specifically prophesy the conversation which would take place when his body was taken to Clonfert.

BRENDAN SENDS HIS SPIRIT TO GOD

He then blessed the brethren and his sister and went to the church with some of his friends and after he had prayed, he sent forth his spirit to God. The journey of his body and the conversation that took place when his body was taken to Clonfert happened exactly as Brendan had prophesied.

Brendan was 93 years old and died in 581 A.D. His body was buried at Clonfert with great honor, amid Psalms and hymns and spiritual songs, in praise of the Father, Son and Holy Spirit.

CUTHBERT OF LINDISFARNE
A.D. 634 - A.D.687 (approx.)

CUTHBERT'S CALL

When Cuthbert was a child he was not interested in anything spiritual. He loved sports and he loved to play. He was always looking for a challenge or a challenger. One day, when he was about eight years old, he was playing a game in a field. A little boy of around three years old ran up to him. The child asked Cuthbert why he was playing and wasting his time on sports when he should be praying and preparing to serve God. When Cuthbert laughed, the little boy threw himself on the ground and began to sob. The other boys tried to console the child but it was no use. Cuthbert also tried to comfort him. The little boy got up and addressed Cuthbert sternly, "Why are you so stubborn in playing these games when God is calling you to serve him?" The child prophesied that one day Cuthbert would be a Bishop. Cuthbert was amazed and then he hugged the child, who immediately stopped crying.

Later on Cuthbert became a shepherd. One night he saw a light streaming from Heaven and he discovered that Aiden, the beloved Bishop of Lindisfarne had died. He immediately took the sheep to their owner and decided to become a monk at the monastery at Melrose.

Cuthbert's life was filled with incredible miracles, including incidents with animals and birds which were fairly common within the early Celtic church.

CUTHBERT AND THE OTTERS

Cuthbert had the habit of leaving the monastery at night. One of the young men (a disciple), wanted to find out where he went when he left the monastery and so he followed him secretly. Cuthbert waded into the river up to his neck and stayed for several hours worshiping and praying. When he came out of the water two otters came to him and stretched themselves out beside him, warming him with the heat of their own bodies. Cuthbert's custom of standing in the water was to keep him awake in order to pray and praise the Lord.

The young man who had followed him was so frightened that he had difficulty making it back to the monastery. When he saw Cuthbert, he fell at his feet asking forgiveness for his spying.

CUTHBERT AND THE BIRDS

Another time when Cuthbert and his servant were traveling and hungry, they prayed for the Lord to send them food. An eagle appeared and brought them a large fish. The servant happily took the fish but Cuthbert asked him, "Why do you not give the fisherman a part too?" Cuthbert proceeded to cut the fish in half and return one half to the eagle.

Later on Cuthbert decided, having left the monastery, that he wanted to emulate the lives of the Desert Fathers, and live by the labor of his own hands. He asked the monks to bring him barley seeds to sow. Having planted the barley, it soon sprang up, but just as it was ripening, some birds flew down and began to eat it. Cuthbert came out and began to scold the birds, "Why are you eating that which you didn't plant? Is it that your need is greater than mine? If so, you have permission to help yourselves; if not, go away, and stop taking that which does not belong to you." The birds left and the barley was harvested. A while later the birds returned and began taking straw from the roof for their nests. Cuthbert again came out and shouted at them, "In the name of Jesus Christ, depart at once; do not dare to cause further damage." When he finished speaking, the birds flew away. Three days later they returned when Cuthbert was digging, and they came and stood in front of him with their heads bowed down. Cuthbert happily forgave them and invited them to return. Next time the birds came back bringing a lump of pig's lard which Cuthbert kept in the guest house for his visitors to grease their shoes. He said, "If the birds can show humility, how much more should we humans seek such virtues." The birds remained on the island with Cuthbert for many years, building nests with materials they found for themselves.

PREACHING

Cuthbert went to many small mountain villages on foot. He was an eloquent preacher. It was said that when he spoke the Word of God his countenance shone with an angelic brightness and the people would begin to confess their sins.

Sometimes at night, in order to stay awake and pray, he would walk around the island. If the other monks complained of being awakened or disturbed in their sleep, he would tell them that they were honored to be awake to praise and magnify the Lord, the Creator.

When he needed to correct someone, tears would course down his cheeks. His zeal for justice was ardent, but his sweetness of disposition and constant joy and peace through a continual closeness to Jesus made him endearing to all those he ministered to.

It was said that Cuthbert's life was one of continual prayer. There was no place, no business, no person, no company which did not offer him a motive to pray. Having prayed all day he would continue into the night hours - which was to him a time of great light and internal delight. He said, "Holy contemplation discovers to the soul a new and most wonderful world whose beauty, riches, and pure delights astonish and transport us out of ourselves." St.Teresa once said, as she came from prayer, that she came from a world more beautiful beyond comparison than a thousand worlds that we behold with our natural eyes.

CUTHBERT GIVES UP HIS SPIRIT

Just prior to his death Cuthbert felt a fire in his stomach and the same day another minister arrived by boat. Cuthbert knew that he was going to be leaving this world and sat down and dictated his final instructions for the brethren. "Live at peace with one another, and when you meet try and agree and be of one mind. Live at peace with those around you and never treat anyone else with contempt. Always welcome others to your monastery. Never imagine that you or your way of life is superior to others, all who share the Christian faith are equal in God's sight."

When he had finished speaking, he was very quiet. In the evening he took communion. As he took the bread he lifted his arms upward as if embracing someone then, his face filled with joy, he gave up his spirit to God.

Note:

Bede says (Bede,hist h.iv.c80) that eleven years after Cuthbert's death, some monks taking up his body, instead of dust which they expected, they found it unputrified with the joints pliable and his clothes fresh. They moved it into a new coffin above the other one.

William of Malmesbury writes (L.4.Pontif.Angl.), The "body was found again incorrupt 415 years later at Durham and publicly shown. During the Danish invasion the monks carried it away from Lindisfarne and after several removals settled with their treasure on a woody hill almost surrounded by the river Were. There they built a church which Aldhune, Bishop of Lindisfarne, dedicated in A.D. 995."

COLUMBA OF IONA
A.D. 521 - A.D. 597

MOCHA'S PROPHESY

Columba was born A.D. 521 at Gartan on the night in which St. Buite (founder of monasteries), died (December 7th). His father, Phelim, was a chieftain of the clan O'Donnell. His mother was Ethne, a descendant of the King of Leinster. He was of royal lineage by both parents.

A disciple of Patrick, Mocha prophesied concerning Columba, "A son is to be born whose name, Columba, will be spread abroad, known through all the provinces of the islands of the ocean, and he shall shed luster upon the last ages of the world. The little fields of our two monasteries shall be separated by the space of one hedge. Columba will be a man very dear to God and of great merit in His sight."

Before the birth of Columba, an angel of the Lord appeared to Columba's mother, Ethne, while she was asleep. Standing by her, he gave her a beautiful mantle (cloak), all the colors of many flowers. After a short while he asked for it back and took it from her hands. Raising it and spreading it out, he sent it forth into the air. Ethne saw the mantle gradually receding from her in flight and increasing in size as to exceed the width of the plains and to overtop the mountains and forests. Ethne, saddened asked, "Why have you taken the lovely mantle away so quickly ?" The angel again said, "Be not saddened, woman, for you will bring forth a son, illustrious and like the prophets of God he will be numbered among them, and will be a leader of innumerable souls to the heavenly country."

Like Brendan, Columba's life is full of eyewitness accounts of his incredible prophetic ministry, accompanied by signs and wonders and angelic visitations (See *Columba - the Celtic Dove* - Kathie Walters).

COLUMBA AND THE DRUID

Columba's monastery in Iona was evangelistic as well as one of teaching, training, prayer and worship. The supernatural realm was a part of everyday life and they expected God to be God. Columba had many confrontations with the druids. In one account Broichan, the druid (from King Brude's court), refused to release a captive slave girl at Columba's request. Columba told him that he would die if he refused. When Columba left the court, Broichan quickly became deathly sick and released the slave girl.

The same druid, Broichan, one day asked Columba when he proposed to sail back to Iona. Columba replied that the third day they would begin the voyage. Broichan answered, "You will not be able to do so, for I will make the wind contrary to you, and bring dark clouds upon you."

On the day of the sailing the shore of Lake Ness was filled with druids, heathen, and Christians who had come to see the outcome of the confrontation between Columba and Broichan. The druids began to rejoice when they saw a dark storm come, and contrary winds in a tempest. Columba called upon the name of the Lord and entered the boat, making the fearful sailors prepare the boat to sail against the wind. The whole crowd watched the boat being borne along, through the contrary wind with amazing velocity and

31

after a short while the adverse winds turned around to the advantage of the voyagers, and to the astonishment of the onlookers.

COLUMBA'S CONFERENCE WITH ANGELS

In one account, Columba instructed the monks to remain behind as he went out to the fields. One young monk followed him, curious as to why Columba wished to be alone. The young man hid behind a small hill and as Columba entered the field, he raised his hands in the air in worship and suddenly many angels came and gathered around him. After a conference with them, Columba turned away and the angels went back to heaven. The curious young monk ran as quickly as he could back to the monastery.

When Columba returned, he sent for the young man and severely rebuked him and charged him to tell no one what he had seen until after his (Columba's) death.

COLUMBA'S REMARKABLE DEATH

Columba had a long and amazing ministry but he longed for the day of his departure to be with the Lord whom he loved and served with all his heart. It is amazing how these early saints had such a rapport with God about their death, which they called their "invitation."

The monks, one day in the monastery of Iona, observed Columba as his face blossomed into a great joy and radiance, his eyes raised to heaven he was filled with great delight. After a few moments, his face became saddened. Pilu, a

Saxon (Englishman), asked the cause of the joy which turned so quickly to sadness. Columba promised that he would tell on the condition that what he said would not be revealed to anyone until after his death, as was his usual custom when telling of the supernatural interventions of the Lord.

Columba said that he had asked the Lord to release him from his time on earth at his thirtieth year (as Abbot of the monastery at Iona). "This was the cause of my rejoicing, I saw the holy angels sent from the throne on high to meet me, but they have been suddenly stopped and are standing on a rock on the other side of the Sound, desirous to approach me. But they have been prevented by the Lord and must soon return to heaven." Columba said that the Lord had yielded to the prayers of many churches in Ireland, and that he was to stay and minister to them for four more years.

After the four years were almost over Columba went to visit the brethren at their work. "During the Easter festival in April, I have desired to pass away to the Lord for He has invited me and granted me this now, but lest your festival of joy be turned into sadness, I put off the day of my departure from this world a little longer." He did not want his death to bring the monks sadness in the midst of the Festival.

Nearer to the time of his departure, and while in the church, Columba's face took on a heavenly glow ("When the heart is glad the countenance blossoms," Prov. 15:13). For he saw the angel of the Lord who had come to take a deposit to heaven - the "deposit" being his soul.

At the end of the same week, Columba and his faithful servant, Diormit, went to bless the fields and granary. Diormit became sad as Columba began to speak of his departing again. "This is the last day for me of this life and this night at midnight, when the Solemn day of the Lord begins, I shall go the way of my fathers, according to the scriptures, for already my Lord Jesus has invited me."

THE WHITE HORSE

After this, returning to the monastery, he stopped to rest half-way and his white horse, a faithful servant, ran up to him and whinnying, laid its head on Columba's breast and shed tears. Diormit began to drive the horse away but Columba forbade him saying, "Let him alone for he loves me. You are a man and possessing a rational soul, you could not know anything about my leaving, except what I have told you myself, but to this beast, devoid of reasoning power, the Creator has Himself clearly revealed to him that his master is about to leave." And he blessed his horse as it turned to go away.

As the joyful hour began to approach, Columba was silent. Then when the bell began to toll at midnight, rising in haste, he ran to the church, where he went to the altar and knelt down in prayer.

THE DEPARTING OF COLUMBA

Diormit, following from a distance, saw the church filled with angelic light, and entering the church he called out, "Where are you father?" and went forward. Finding

Columba lying on the floor, he sat down and laid Columba's head in his lap. Meanwhile the whole community of monks came running up with lights, and began to weep at the sight of their dying Father. Those who were present reported, "Columba looked around with face upturned, with wonderful cheerfulness and great joy of countenance on seeing the holy angels come to meet him. Diormit then lifted up Columba's hands that he might bless the monks. And he then gave up his spirit to God. After his spirit had left his body, his countenance remained ruddy and gladdened, like one living and not dead, for many hours," (*Life of St. Columba*- Adamnan 1922).

Luguid, in Ireland, had a vision of a great light streaming from heaven into Iona and knew that Columba was going to be with the Lord. Fishermen on the shores of Ireland also saw the light streaming from heaven down upon the island of Iona at the time Columba departed.

Before his death Columba had prophesied that crowds of people would not be allowed by God to come to Iona for the funeral offices and although many people wanted to come, they were prevented by a great tempest of wind. After the funeral, the tempest ceased.

From Original *The Life of St. Columba* - Adamnan. *Columba-The Celtic Dove* - Kathie Walters

BRIGID - FIRST ABBESS OF KILDARE
A.D. 453 - A.D. 524

BRIGID

Born about the middle of the fifth century, Brigid's first miracle happened the same day she was born. A baby boy had been birthed the day previously and the child had died. Somehow little Brigid had been brought into contact with this dead child and as she happened to touch the dead baby, life came back into him.Those present immediately declared it to be a sign to confirm some prophesies about the coming of Brigid. The dead infant was said to be the son of the King of Connaille, who was then on a visit.

FLAMES

One day, Brigid's mother, while working in a field had left the baby asleep in the house. Suddenly it appeared that flames were engulfing the cradle and those around ran to extinguish them. As they entered the room the flames went out and they found Brigid sweetly sleeping and smiling, with a rosy hue flushing her face. All proclaimed aloud the child was anointed with the graces of the Holy Spirit.

SLAVE GIRLS

In the Ireland of Brigid's day there is no evidence of injustice or subjection for most women, although another class, the bondmaids or slave-girls were less fortunate. They had no rights and many were badly treated. Adamnan's Law recounts the injustices these girls suffered. When they became Christians they had problems, as their masters did not expect them to live up to a high moral code. Slave girls were the property, body and soul of their owners. St. Patrick pitied them profoundly and made mention of them specially in his *Confession*, "Women who are kept in slavery suffer especially. They constantly endure even terrors and threats. But the Lord gave grace to many of His handmaidens, for although they are forbidden, they earnestly follow the example set them."

Christianity became extremely inconvenient to these masters, as those slaves who followed Christ wanted to stay with their families, whereas the masters would often sell the wife or husband to someone far away. Children would be sold to others and brought up without any knowledge of their parents. This was the kind of stage that was set for the appearance of Brigid.

It was into this environment Brigid was born. It is believed by some that her actual birthplace was at Faughart, two miles from Dundalk in County Louth and was about 453 A.D. Her father was Dubthach, a pagan petty king or chieftain, and her mother was a Christian bondwoman named Brocessa, who belonged to his household. This is from the account given in three of the six *Lives* contained in Colgan's, *Triadis Thaumaturegae*.

"Even before her birth there was a jealousy present in Brigid's life in the form of Dubthach's wife who forced him to sell Brocessa to a distant buyer - a druid who lived westward in Connaugh. As was the custom, offspring were reserved to the original owner, which meant that when Brigid was old enough to be useful, she was claimed back into Dubthach's household and assumed her mother's role, grinding corn, washing the feet of the guests, tending the sheep etc."

NAMING "BRIGID"

Brocessa had no rights, but over the bed where the bondmaid slept, a flame and fiery pillar was seen. There were also three evil spirits who came, *Servitude, Injustice* and *Envy*. Three angels in shining white came to banish them and confirm the babe's name - Brigid. When Brigid was old enough to be useful, she was then transferred back to Dubthach's household where she carried out the daily routine. But she was capable also of sudden, disconcerting gestures. When a beggar came for alms, she would give him a sheep from the flock. Once, five guests arrived and she was given five pieces of bacon to cook, but the dog, licking her hand, looked imploringly at her and so she gave him a piece. As her master's wrath was breaking out, five pieces of bacon were found again in the pot. There were many occasions when she gave food and other items from the master's house, and then supernatural intervention occurred to make up the losses of her owner.

Finally Dubthach's wife, still jealous, demanded that he sell Brigid. Dutchach took her in his chariot and informed her that he was selling her to the King of Leinster, baptized a Christian by Patrick.

THE SEVEN KINGDOMS OF IRELAND

Ireland was split into seven kingdoms, Ailech, Airgialla, Ulaid in the north. (Roughly modern Ulster) Connacht, then Mide and Laigin (Approximately Modern Leinster) and Mumu (Munster). Each of these kingdoms was further sub-divided into lesser kingdoms, ruled over by sub-kings. The sub-kings were ruled by, and owed tribute and war service to the overlords or kings, who were in turn were ruled by the High King of Ireland.

There were rivalries and coalitions arising and shifting among the seven kingdoms, which were sometimes further divided by domestic feuds. During Brigid's lifetime there are listed fifteen internal wars with three main causes of strife. One was over boundaries and lands. The second was among the Ui Neill family group over possession of the High King's throne. The third contention was because of a tax that had been levied on Leinster (Boramha). It was levied to avenge an insult to the High King's daughters.

THE TRAVELING MINISTERS

The traveling ministers, like Patrick, often had to pay heavy sums for their safe-conduct through contending states. One report of Patrick's says, "*On occasion, I would give presents to the kings, beside the hire that I gave to their sons who accompany me; nevertheless, they seized me with my companions. And on that day they most eagerly desired to kill me, but my time had not yet come. And everything they found with us they plundered, and me myself they bound with irons. And on the fourteenth day the Lord delivered me from their power. Moreover, you know by proof how much I paid to those who were judges throughout all the districts which I frequented most, for I reckon that I distributed to them not less than the price of fifteen men, so that ye might enjoy me. Daily I expect either slaughter or to be defrauded, or reduced to slavery, or to an unfair attack of some kind"* (Patrick's -*Confession*).

DUBTHACH'S SWORD

Taking Brigid to be sold to the King of Leinster, Dubthach arrived and left Brigid in the chariot while he went to haggle over the price with the king. He placed his sword on the seat near her. Then a leper appeared at the side of the chariot begging for alms. Unlike other countries, the lepers in Ireland were not treated as outcasts but rather, because of their misfortune, were privileged members of society. As a result they often became impudent to a degree. Irish lepers went about freely, were compassionately tolerated, received bountiful alms and liberal medical succor - not especially hygienic, but exceedingly humane. When Brigid saw the face looking at her with mournful eyes, she gave the only thing near her, which was Dubthach's sword.

At that very moment the King of Leinster was asking the chieftain why he wanted to sell the child, and Dubthach was explaining that he could not keep her because of her open-handedness to the poor, saying that nothing was safe in her keeping. Upon his return, and finding his sword missing he was "mightily enraged" as told by the old *Life*. Brigid was taken before the king who having become a Christian, was nearer to understanding her. Poor Dubthach's bad day reached a climax when the king said, "Leave her alone, for her merit before God is greater than ours." Brigid was taken back home by her father .

BRIGID'S REJECTION OF A HUSBAND

On her return from a visit to her mother, Dubthach made one more attempt to order his daughters life by arranging a marriage to, "A man of chaste life and a poet," (*Irish Lives.*) In those days a poet was given large amounts of money and was an important fellow. He was often in the king's court. Brigid would have none of it. She not only rejected marriage, but the whole idea of it, she decided to become a virgin for Christ. She had a part in the beginnings of a great movement toward monasticism, which St. Patrick found so astonishing. The Apostle wrote in his *Confession*, "See how in Ireland there has lately been formed a people of the Lord, sons and daughters of Irish chieftains are seen to become monks and nuns and their number increases more and more. They do it," he tells us, "Not with the consent of their fathers, but they endure persecution and lying reproaches from their kindred."

It was Brigid who saved the women's ascetic movement by the innovation of community life. She began the organization of women. When she appeared for ordination, she had seven others with her. These eight seem never to have separated.

BRIGID-THE NUN

As a nun, Brigid dressed in white with her hair uncut. She did not live an enclosed life. Going into a convent for her meant becoming one of the most traveled people in the land. This monastic movement in the 5-6th century expressed itself in the most strenuous apostolic work for souls. The church hierarchy that Patrick established consisted of various bishops under the primacy of Armagh. These bishops seemed to have received Brigid without hesitancy, on terms of equality.

THE COLUMN OF FIRE

As Brigid was officially received by the bishops, a column of fire descended over her head and was seen by the assistants of the church. She rested her hand for an instant on the edge of the wooden altar and all that part of the dry seasoned timber became green. One intimate of Patrick's, Bishop Erc of Slane, became a devout friend of Brigid. Erc afterwards became Bishop of Ardfert in Kerry and was a tutor to the great navigator-saint, Brendan. Many of Brigid's chariot journeys were undertaken at the direction of Bishop Erc. He brought her on a tour of Munster in order to personally help her to establish new foundations in his territory. Besides Munster, she traveled over the whole of Ireland.

THE FAMOUS CONVENT AT KILDARE

The most famous of Brigid's foundations and the crown of her labors was her Leinster convent at Kildare. It was the reigning King of Leinster who gave her the site. Brigid set up here a great religious center, modeled on the settlements of Patrick. Often when a pagan king was converted, he would donate a settlement. Brigid's foundations were very successful, and quite prosperous. All the bishops of Ireland wanted her to found convents in their districts.

Brigid once requested of Aillill, a Leinster chieftain, some wattles for building a settlement at Kildare. Aillill had prepared the wattles (poles used for laying a thatch roof) for his own house and refused Brigid's request. Suddenly all the horses fell to the ground and nothing would induce them to get up again. In the end he left the wattles for Brigid.

The Kildare foundation rapidly grew to such magnitude that it became as large as a city and a bishop had to be appointed to the territory. Many wonderful things were made at Kildare and they poured forth over Ireland. Bells, croziers, chalices, book-rests and Kildare's special products - manuscripts which became very famous. One description by the twelfth century historian, Giraldus Cambrensis, says of one of the manuscripts -*The book of Kildare*, "Delicate and ingenious, so artful, so involved and interlaced and illuminated with colors still so fresh, and truly you would say these were all combined by the diligence of an angel rather than of a man. For my part, the more often and carefully I look upon it, I am ever astonished anew. I ever find food for wonderment."

We tend to think of the monasteries and convents in terms of poverty, but they were prosperous. Cogitosus wrote a description of the church and tombs of Brigid and Conlaeth, about one hundred years after Brigid's death, "The tombs were lavishly decorated with gold and silver and gems. A crown of gold hung over Brigid's tomb and a crown of silver over Conlaeth's." He says that the church was very spacious and lofty with a richly decorated interior. Tapestry and paintings extended though the sanctuary.

FINNIAN

Finnian of Leinster was the founder of Clonard, the monastery / school that outrivaled Kildare. Finnian had as many as three thousand students and a hundred bishops in charge of them. He was called the, "Tutor of the Saints of Ireland." But he took counsel together with Brigid. Brendan asked Brigid one time how she so powerfully prevailed with God. She replied that her mind was never detached from God.

A feature of this Celtic Christianity was the ideally friendly relationship between the monastic settlements. Adamnan's *The Life of St. Columba,* in particular abounds with examples of affection between the early fathers. When one visited the settlement of another, he was always received joyfully and with honor. They exchanged gifts; they entertained each other. If they were fasting, they would cease the fast in order to celebrate the arrival of a guest.

THE MIRACLE OF THE MUSIC

Brigid loved music and one time at a chieftain's fortress, somewhere near Knockaney (County Limerick), Brigid went to ask for the release of a captive. She was asked to sit and wait for the chieftain by the man's aged foster-father. While she was waiting, she saw some harps hanging on the wall. She asked for some music but the harpists were not there. The sisters with Brigid told the foster-father to take the harp, and while Brigid was present he would be able to play. The old man took down the harp from the wall, thrummed it clumsily, but suddenly found he could produce airs and harmonies. Another of the household anxiously tried a second harp with the same result.

Presently the place was filled with happy music and the chieftain arrived home to hear it. He heard rare laughter from his foster-father. Pleased with his homecoming he conceded to Brigid all that she asked.

BRIGID'S GIVING

Brigid gave and gave and gave again. Everything she was given she gave away. The *Irish Lives* are crowded with accounts of the miraculous events in her life and some of them are humorous, for example; two robbers stole some cattle from her fields at night time. They took the cattle to the river to cross over. But the cattle became stubborn and would not budge. The thieves shouted and hit them to no avail and finally they decided on a plan. They removed their clothes, which they tied to the animal's horns and plunged into the river dragging the cattle after them. This worked until they got to midstream, when the cattle suddenly turned around and bolted back to the bank, clothes still on the horns. When the sun arose, the farm workers were amazed to see naked men running along the river bank.

Another time Brigid saw a man passing by her gates carrying a sack on his back. "What are you carrying?" she asked, knowing that it was much needed salt. "Stones," said the man who did not want to give up any of his salt. "Stones? Let it be," she replied. The man's knees began to buckle under a new weight. He stumbled back to Brigid whose word he now feared. "What have you in that sack?" she asked again. "Salt," he replied, "Let it be," said Brigid. And immediately it was salt.

Brigid's sole recreation was hospitality, everyone who came to her doors was received. Her only concern was that she have enough for everyone.

BRIGID AND THE FOX

Most of the Celtic Christians exercised great authority over animals. Brigid, like Ciaran, once tamed a fox. A bondman was cutting trees in a wood when he accidentally killed a pet fox belonging to the King of Leinster. The fox was able to do several tricks and the king was very fond of it. He was furious with the servant and, in anger, decreed the man's death. The news was brought to Brigid because she had favor with the king. She set out in her chariot and on the way she saw a fox and called out to it. It immediately sprang into the cart and nestled against her feet. Caressing it, she dismounted and she commanded it to follow her and it trotted obediently behind her. Within the fortress, the king was still angry at the loss of his pet. Brigid called the fox, fresh from the woods, and began to put it through some tricks before a delighted household. The animal responded to her voice and she offered it to the king. Being placated, he released the prisoner. The following day the fox ran away - back to the woods.

BRIGID AND THE FOOL

Another time, a smart young man who was well off, thought Brigid was a fool and decided to prove it. He disguised himself and joined the beggars who crowded around Brigid every morning when she left the monastery to go to the fields. He begged a sheep and she gave him one. He came on several other occasions with disguises, joining in with the crowd of beggars. In this way he obtained five sheep from Brigid. His own flock of course increased and he laughed at the thought of Brigid's decreased flock. But after his last visit, he found that the extra sheep were missing from his flock the next morning. Brigid's flock was increased by five! The sheep left and returned to Brigid's flock.

HOSPITALITY

Hospitality was a very great emphasis of the monasteries. The Abbot Conan transferred his whole monastery to another place when he realized it was somewhat inaccessible to travelers. Truly the hospitality and entertainment extended to travelers was extravagant. Brigid hated formalism and legalism. One time during Lent when she and the other nuns were fasting, they became short on supplies because of a previous failed harvest, and they made a journey to another monastery which was under Abbot Ibar. They arrived famished and exhausted. All that was available was bacon and bread. As they sat down Brigid heartily gave thanks to God for the food. The other nuns however made a point of refaining from the bacon. "Well we're going to keep the Lent fast, whatever you may do." With that Brigid got angry and threw them out of the room.

REVELATION OF BRIGID'S DEATH

Four years before her death Brigid received a revelation from the Holy Spirit that the time of her departure was approaching. She also had prophetic foreknowledge of her place of resurrection. This gave her great joy. She had a great desire to visit the tomb of Patrick before she died, but she knew that she would not return to her own place. Before Patrick died, he had instructed Brigid to bless all Ireland before she departed. This she set out to do.

Brigid gave charge of her flock to her dear friend and fellow-laborer, Darlugdacha, prophesying to her that she would survive Brigid for one year and die on the same day (1st February).

When Brigid entered joyfully into the arms of the Lord Jesus, Communion was ministered to her by Ninnid - the pure-handed. It was said that she prophesied this event to him when he was a young boy.

PATRICK - THE CELTIC LION
A.D.398 - A.D. 471

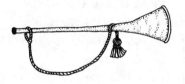

THE SPIRITUAL BREASTPLATE OF ST. PATRICK

It is said that Patrick prayed this prayer every morning:

"I bind myself today to the strong Name of the Trinity,
By invocation of the same, the Three-in-One,
and One-in-Three.

I bind this day to me forever, by the power of faith, Christ's
Incarnation;
His baptism in the river Jordan;
His death on the Cross for my salvation;
His bursting forth from the spiced tomb;
His riding up the heavenly way;
His coming at the day of doom.

I bind myself unto the power of the great love of the
Cherubim; The sweet, "Well done," in judgment hour;
The service of the Seraphim;
Confessor's faith, Apostle's word;
The Patriarch's prayers, the Prophet's scrolls;
All good deeds done unto the Lord.

I bind myself today to the virtues of the starlit heaven;
The glorious sun's life-giving ray;
The whiteness of the moon at even;
The flashing of the lightening free;
The whirling wind's tempestuous shocks;

I bind myself today to the power of God to hold and lead;
His eye to watch; His might to stay.
The wisdom of my God to teach;
His hand to guide; His shield to ward;
The Word of God to give me speech;
His heavenly host to be my guard, against the demon snares
of sin;
The natural lusts that war within;
The hostile men that mar my course:
Few or many, far or nigh;
In every place and in all hours;
Against their fierce hostility.

I bind to me these Holy powers against all Satan's spells
and wiles; against false words of heresy:
Against the knowledge that defiles:
Against the heart's idolatry;
Against the wizard's evil craft;
Against the death-wound and the burning;
The choking wave and the poisoned shaft;
Protect me, Christ, 'til thy returning.

Christ be with me, Christ within me;
Christ beside me, Christ before me, Christ behind me,
Christ to win me, Christ beneath me, Christ above me;
Christ in quiet, Christ in danger;
Christ in hearts of all that love me;
Christ in the mouth of friend and stranger.

I bind unto myself the strong name of the Trinity;
By invocation of the same, The Three-in-one,
and One-in-Three;
Of whom all nature hath creation. Eternal Father,
Word and Spirit.

Praise to the Lord of my salvation.

PATRICK'S CHILDHOOD

Patrick was born of Christian parents toward the close of the fourth century. His father, Calpurnius, though of British race, was by birth a Roman citizen, and held the rank, Decurion. The father and grandfather of Calpurnias, Potitus and Odissus, had both been Christians; so that the family had kept the faith for at least several generations. Conchessa, Patrick's mother, was a near relative of the great St. Martin of Tours. She was a wise and good woman, and sought to bring up their children in the fear and love of God.

As the son of a Roman Citizen, and a British noble, Patrick was bound to have had some education. According to the custom of British citizens of the Roman Empire, Patrick was given three names, rendered in Latin as Patricius, Magonus, Sacatus. Patricius meaning, 'noble', and Sacatus, a Celtic word meaning, 'valiant in war'.

Patrick had a brother, Sannan, and five sisters. They all became servants of God and the church. Calpurnius lived at Bannavem Taberniae, which was near the rock of

Dumbarton, or in Wales. It was certainly in some part of Roman Britain or Brittany.

The fact that St. Patrick worked great and wonderful miracles is beyond question, and those miracles won him enthusiastic admiration and enduring love of the people.

De Vere wrote long ago of Patrick:

"Beholding not alone his wondrous works,
But, wondrous more, the sweetness of his strength,
And how he neither shrank from flood nor fire,
And how he couched him on the wintry rocks,
and how he sang great hymns to One who heard,
And how he cared for poor men and the sick,
And for the souls, invisible to men."

PATRICK'S BAPTISM

Miracles happened over the birth of Patrick. As no priest was to be found, the infant was taken to the blind hermit, Gornias, to be baptized. A difficulty arose because there was no water to perform the ceremony. Gornias however, by faith, took the baby's hand and with it traced the sign of the cross upon the earth, and as a result, water gushed forth. Bathing his own eyes the hermit saw, and he then baptized Patrick.

From his childhood he had been able to understand the things of God. Patrick, in his *Book of Epistles*, said, "And God had pity on my youth and ignorance, and He took care of me before I knew Him, and before I could distinguish between good and evil. And He strengthened me and comforted me as a father does his son. "

PATRICK'S FOSTERING

Fostering was a custom peculiar to the tribal system of ancient Ireland and was regulated by the Brehon laws, which ordained that the sons of nobles should be educated in the homes of the tribesmen until they reached the age of seventeen - the daughters until their fourteenth year.

Although of noble birth, Patrick was not brought up in luxury. Patrick's foster-parents are represented as careful, thrifty people, perhaps living on the farm which belonged to Calpurnius, and attending to his flocks and herds.

MIRACLES IN PATRICK'S CHILDHOOD

At one time when he was out playing in the ice and snow, Patrick took some icicles in his jacket and ran with them to his foster mother, thinking that she would be pleased. She was irritated and told him that it would better to bring a piece of wood for the fire. Patrick smiled sweetly and told her to trust God and the icicles would start a fire. Very soon a fire was roaring on the hearth.

Once when Patrick was minding sheep with his little sister, Lupita, she tripped and fell, striking her head against a stone. Her brother was some distance away, but when he returned and found her laying unconscious, he prayed over her and raised her up. The wound was instantly healed and the girl recovered.The scar remained visible, as a proof of the miracle. The children returned home together as if nothing had happened.

On one occasion when the Britons had a meeting, his foster-parents took him along with them. While they were there his foster-father suddenly collapsed and died. At first a great hush fell upon the assembly and then the man's relatives began to weep and his wife cried, and calling to Patrick she said, "My boy, why have you allowed the man who has been so kind to you to die?" Patrick had been playing with the other children and had not noticed the distress of the people. But seeing what had happened he ran to his foster-father and putting his arm round the dead man's neck, he said affectionately, "Get up and let us go home." The man arose and returned home with his wife and boys.

SOLD AS A SLAVE

When Patrick was sixteen years old the Picts and Scots began to raid the coast, plunder and take hostages. One of the most victorious of these sea kings, was Niall, surnamed, "Of the Nine Hostages," (because he took hostages from nine places). It was during one of Niall's raids that Patrick was taken as a slave along with a maidservant, his sister, Lupita, and some other companions.

He was taken by ship to Ireland, somewhere along the coast of Antrim and sold to a petty king, Milcho. He was put in charge of a herd of swine and spent most time out in the fields. But it was there that God was made real to him, and as he said later, his eyes were opened to see his unbelief, and he was truly converted. All the scripture which he learned as a child flooded his mind and heart and he decided that somehow he would become a servant of God.

Milcho was so impressed with Patrick that he asked him to teach his children to read. But Milcho was a druid and opposed to Christianity, which was spreading across Ireland. Patrick had many conversations with the angel of Ireland, named Victor.

VICTOR, THE ANGEL, GIVES INSTRUCTION TO PATRICK

One night after six years, he heard the voice of the angel, Victor, who was standing near. He said, "Soon you will return to your country." A while later, Victor spoke to him again, "Your ship is ready." Patrick managed to escape, and trusting God, he made his way to the coast. After a few days he found a ship ready to sail, and was taken on board.

Eventually Patrick, after months of journeying, arrived home. His parents had died but his relatives welcomed him. One night he was awakened by the angel, Victor, whom he had known in Ireland. He was standing beside Patrick's bed holding many letters in his hand, Victor selected one and handed it to Patrick. It read, *"The Voice of the Irish."* Then he heard many voices calling to him to come back to Ireland and bring the message of the Gospel.

Although the angel, Victor said, "Go to Ireland, for you shall be an Apostle of its people," Patrick determined to go to Rome to lay his case before the Bishop. However, he met Germanus first and he was ordained by him. There is some confusion as to whether Patrick actually went to see Bishop Celestine in Rome or not. But the angel came to him while he was with Germanus and said, "You are commanded by God to go to Ireland, to strengthen their faith and belief, and that you may bring the Irish by the net of the Gospel to the harbor of life." And so Patrick bade farewell to Germanus who gave him a blessings and sent one of his servants, a minister Segetius, to help and testify for him.

PATRICK AND KIERAN

During Patrick's time with Germanus, he met and prophesied to Kieran who was on his way from Rome. He told Kieran that he would go before him to Ireland and be Abbot over a monastery in Saigher. Patrick gave him a bell which he said would ring when he came to a certain fountain where he was to build his church and monastery.

PATRICK RETURNS TO IRELAND

Finally Patrick returned to Ireland in A.D. 432. The ministry to the Irish began, not without opposition from the druids and wizards who tried desperately to keep Patrick away from the kings. Patrick believed that if the kings could be won for God then the people would follow.

THE BATTLE ON THE HILL OF TARA

One of the first spiritual battles between Patrick and the druids was fought at the Hill of Tara, in A.D. 433. The High King, Laeghaire (Leary), son of the renowned Niall of the Nine Hostages, had invited the sub-kings and nobles and bards to a lavish festival. It was to start with great bonfires but until the first ceremonial fire was lit by the Chief druid, it was forbidden for other fires to be seen.

King Laeghaire, in his efforts to hold his power over the lower kings had given himself to the power of the wizards and skillful magicians and druidic priests along with their idols. Lochru and Lucat-Mael were his chief wizards. Being false prophets they had foretold that, "An evil teacher would come from over the sea to their land and that a multitude would receive him, and that he would find love and reverence from the men of Ireland." They said, "He would cast out from their realms the evil kings and lords and would destroy all the idols, and that the worship established by him would abide in the land forever."

No doubt the druids knew of the progress of Christianity in Britain and Europe. Their brethren abroad had been discredited and they were afraid of the same fate. They were very much afraid of losing their influence and authority.

Patrick, leaving the friendly hospitality of Dichu, sailed southward and arrived at Inver Colptha, the mouth of the river Boyne. They followed the course of the stream for about 12 miles until they came to the Hill of Slane where Patrick proposed to celebrate Easter.

While they rested there on the hill, they saw the magnificent view of the river Boyne; to the north, far away were the purple mountains of Mourne, and to the south lay the beautiful hills of Wicklow. Against this background, about

10 miles away, stood the Royal Hill of Tara. The roofs of the palace were shining in the setting sun.

PATRICK'S FIRE

When the sun had set, Patrick prepared to begin the celebration of the Resurrection of Christ. It was the first time the Paschal fire was lit, never to be extinguished in the land. Hardly were the Christian torches seen to blaze, when the attention of the high king was drawn to the scene. The whole of Mag Breg (the Beautiful Plain), was illuminated by the fires, while Tara was still in darkness. Angrily, the king called his attendants and told them to find out who had dared to light the fires and break the law he had made for the occasion of the festivals of Beltane and Samhain.

The druids told King Laeghaire that there was no need to send messengers to Slane for they knew what the fires were. "We see the fire," they said, "And we know that unless it is quenched on the night in which it is made, it will never be quenched for ever. The man who kindled it will vanquish the kings and lords of Ireland unless he is forbidden." "This shall not be!" cried the king, "But we will go down and kill this man who made the fires."

Meanwhile on the Hill of Slane, Patrick had begun with the others the celebration of the Easter festival, singing and worshiping God.

It was late when nine chariots bearing the king and queen with two chief druids, and a number of nobles came thundering toward Slane. The wizards began to fear that the king might fail by taking a hasty action. As they drew toward the Christians, the druid wizards spoke to King Laeghaire, "You should be careful," they cautioned the king, "Not to go down to the place where the fire was made and give any respect to the man who kindled the fire. Stay outside and have him brought out to you, so that he will know that you are the king, and he is the subject." The king was flattered and agreed.

They drove to the place called, "The Graves of Fiacc's Men," and they un-yoked the horses. The king and his nobles sat in solemn state, and the warriors stood with their shields erect in front of them. In the light of the fires they looked very fierce. The king forbade anyone to rise to greet Patrick or any of his company (contrary to the custom of the Irish). A messenger was sent to fetch Patrick.

Soon a bright procession appeared descending the hill. As Patrick advanced, all eyes were fixed on him. Calmly he sang as he approached the king, "Some trust in chariots, and some in horses; but we will call upon the Name of the Lord our God."

As Patrick's clear strong voice resounded, a feeling of awe filled the minds of the warriors. One man, Erc, the son of Deg, rose to greet Patrick. By grace, in a moment he believed in God and Patrick blessed him. Later on he was baptized and eventually became the first Bishop of Slane. Patrick prophesied to him, "Your city on earth will be high and noble."

THE DRUID'S DEFEAT

After a formal greeting between Laeghaire and Patrick, the wizard Lochru attacked him angrily with contention and shouting. He became malicious and hostile and even violent, blaspheming the Holy Trinity. Patrick's anger was roused and he called upon God, "O Lord, Who can do all things and on Whose power everything depends. You have sent us here to preach Your Name to the heathen. Now let this ungodly man, who blasphemes your Name, be lifted up and let him die." No sooner had Patrick finished speaking than a supernatural force raised the wizard in the air. He fell heavily down, his head striking a stone. And so he died in the presence of those assembled.

The heathen seeing their own subdued, and realizing that Patrick had more power than the druids, were greatly affected. But the king was enraged at the fate of Lochru, on whom he had depended. He then wanted to take the life of Patrick. "Slay this man," he cried to his guards.

But Patrick stood firmly in his place. With flashing eyes and resonant voice he said, "Let God arise and His enemies be scattered. Let them that hate Him, flee from before His face! As smoke vanishes, so let them vanish away: as wax melts before the fire, so let the wicked perish at the presence of God."

THE EARTHQUAKE

By this time the sun had begun to rise and the morning splendor bathed the earth. But at the words of Patrick, darkness crept back over the sky and the ground shook with an earthquake.

The swords and spears of the warriors clashed against their shields and it seemed to them that the sky was falling down, and there was no hope of escape from impending destruction. The frightened horses galloped away in confusion, and the wind blew so fiercely that the chariots were physically moved.

Because of the confusion and fear, the warriors fled, leaving only three people with King Laeghaire and Queen Angas. The king remained sullen and silent but the queen rose and approached Patrick. She spoke to him with respect. "Just and mighty man," she said, "Do not destroy the king. He will come to you and he will do your will and he will kneel and believe in your God." Her influence prevailed and because the events of the past few hours had shaken him, the king kneeled before Patrick, offering peace. It was a false gesture, designed to allow him to avoid the present situation.

INVITATION TO TARA

Laeghaire designed a plan in his mind to try and kill Patrick on the way to his castle. "Follow after me, to my castle, Cleric," said the wily king, "And at Tara I may believe in your God in the presence of the men of Ireland."

THE KING'S TRAP

Patrick consented and Laeghaire gave orders to his servants that an ambush should be set on several paths between Slane and Tara. The chariots were yoked once more by the attendant who had now returned, and the royal party set out back to the palace. They were very weary and discouraged after their disastrous night with Patrick.

THE KING'S BANQUET

Patrick and his company continued the interrupted Easter Day celebration with hearts full of gratitude to God. Then Patrick selected his companions and blessed them before setting out for Tara. There were eight young clerics, including Patrick and the boy, Benignus, who never left Patrick's side. They had ten miles to walk, but God covered them with a cloak of darkness so that they could not be seen. God had revealed to Patrick the evil design of the king.

The king's servants watched but they saw only eight deer and a young fawn. It was after this that Patrick wrote his famous hymn, *The Deer's Cry*, in which he gave God praise and expressed his firm belief in the resurrection, the incarnation and, death and ascension of Christ. He declared glory to God, who was his defense against the wiles of the devil and against all forms of superstition and idolatry; ending with an appeal to Christ to be with him always and speak to him through every creature.

When Patrick arrived at the banquet hall, King Laeghaire and his dignitaries were already seated. Patrick waited to see who would rise to greet him. It would have been considered an insult to refrain from rising upon the entrance of a guest, especially one who had been invited personally by the king.

The man who did rise was the king's poet, Dubthach, and a younger man named Fiacc. They both later became disciples. Although everyone else including King Laeghaire was very angry with Patrick because his words has caused the death of the king's druid, Patrick stood firm and confident. The other druid-wizard, Lucat-mael, still very bitter because of the death of his comrade, Lochru, and wanting to please the king, poisoned Patrick's cup. Patrick, aware that most of the people at the king's court would want him dead, had already prayed on the way to the castle.

Patrick blessed all that he ate and drank in the Name of the Lord and the poison had no ill-effect.

ANOTHER BATTLE WITH THE DRUIDS

King Laeghaire had decided that there would be an open "competition" between Patrick and his God and the druids and their demonic power. This was to take place at the bottom of the hill.

Lucat first proposed that they both try to bring snow upon the plains and Patrick said he had no desire to go against the will of God. Lucat said that he didn't care at all what Patrick's God wanted, he was going to bring the snow and demonstrate the power of his gods. Because of his unwillingness, Lucat believed that snow was not among Patrick's collection of miracles.

Very soon, as Lucat chanted and prayed, snow fell all around the people. Patrick then said to him, "Now get rid of the snow." Lucat confessed that he was unable. "In evil does your power lie," said Patrick, and raising his right arm, he blessed the plain in the Name of the Lord Jesus. The snow immediately melted.

The druid was disconcerted and he brought forth thick clouds of darkness. "Now dispel the darkness," said Patrick. But he could not. Patrick again blessed the plain and the dark clouds rolled away.

After several other manifestations of druid magic, the king saw that his wizard was losing the battle and then proposed that the druid books and the Christian books be cast into the stream which flowed down the hill. Patrick was willing but the druid was not. "He has water as a god," he said (he was referring to the rite of baptism). "Then throw them into the fire," said the king. But again the wizard would not. "He also venerates the god of fire" (he had heard of the fire of the Holy Spirit). Patrick finally decided to put an end to the demonstrations and suggested they both be put into separate huts and shut in, and the huts set alight. Seeing there was no escape from the decision and as he already was humiliated, Lucat agreed.

THE FIRE

The huts were set ablaze and Patrick like the children in the fiery furnace, was unharmed. The wizard, of course, died in the flames.

Great was the anger of King Laeghaire when he saw he was deprived of his second druid wizard. He would have liked to kill Patrick himself but he was prevented by the Spirit of God. "Unless you believe now, you will die quickly," Patrick said to the king. King Laeghaire was seized with fear and went aside to his council-chamber and said to his officers, "In my opinion it is better to serve Patrick's God than for me to die presently." And so the king once more bowed before Patrick. Many thousands that day were baptized as a result. Patrick went in peace to the king's court and was met with hostility. He stood firm in the power of God as he had done the day previously, and as a result King Laeghaire gave protection to the Christians in his own kingdom, although he was never truly converted himself.

PATRICK CONVERTS DUBLIN

As Patrick came near to Dublin, at that time a small village, he prophesied, "That village which is now very small shall hereafter become very eminent. It shall be enlarged in riches and dignity. Neither shall it cease to grow until it has become the principal seat of all the kingdom."

When the people of Dublin heard of the great signs and miracles that were done through Patrick, and when they saw him coming near to their village, they went out to meet him.

At this time, Alphinus was King of Dublin. He and all the citizens were in great sorrow over the death of the king's two children. His only son, Eochadh, had died of a sickness in his bedroom. His daughter had just been drowned in the adjoining river now known as the Liffey. She had ventured into the deep part for the purpose of bathing. The young lady's body was drawn out of the waters after some considerable search, and laid by her brother's corpse, in order that their funeral rites might be solemnized together. The tombs were prepared according to the superstition of the pagans. In the meantime news was spread over all the city that, "Patrick, the potent reviver of many dead persons," had been seen near the town. For Jesus, who burst asunder the gates of death and of hell, smoothed the way for his servant. The king and the people who before had said to the Lord, "Depart from us, we will not acknowledge any of thy ways," were so cast down; saddened with grief, that all of their rebellion and all their barbarous rudeness, and all the pride and idolatry was utterly subdued.

PATRICK'S CHALLENGE

The king, hearing of St. Patrick's arrival, greatly rejoiced and asked him to come in to where his two children lay dead. He then promised, before all those present, that if God restored his children to life, he and all the citizens would become Christians. Seeing such a gain of souls in the sight of the king, his nobles, and all the common people,

Patrick raised from death to life those princely children. Their bodily resurrection attributed greatly toward the spiritual resurrection of their father and the rest of his people. The king and all his subjects, being astonished at this great miracle, turned away from the worship of idols and they were baptized in the spring.

From that day the king and all the people worshiped God and gave liberally to Patrick, so that he was able to give to the poor in that place and other places and have enough to build churches.

(Ref: *Ecclesiastical History of Ireland*, *Rev. Dr. Lanigan. Sexta Vita S. Patricii, Joycelin notes.*)

PATRICK AND THE KING'S DAUGHTER, PATRICK'S FAST, AND PETITIONS FOR IRELAND 434 A.D.

Patrick and his companions arrived in the early morning at Tulsk, in the county of Roscommon. As they sat down near the fountain known as Clibach they were approached by the two daughters of one of the kings of Ireland. They were intending to bathe in the fountain. Seeing the young clerics with their books in front of them, the young women wondered at the strange sight so early in the morning.

The two women, Eithne and Feidelm, inquired of Patrick as to what race he was of and from where he had recently come. "Are you some kind of gods?" asked Eithne. "It is better for you to ask about our God than to inquire as to our race," said Patrick. "Where is God to be found? Is He under the earth? Or in the streams? Or in the hills and valleys?" asked Eithne. "Is He beautiful and to be loved? How is He to be found?" she continued.

Patrick, full of the Holy Spirit replied, "Our God is the God over all; over heaven and earth: the God of the seas and rivers: the God of the sun and moon and stars: the God of the high mountains and lowly valleys; He quickens all things; He gives the light to the sun and moon; He created the waters in dry land; He places islands in the middle of the sea and He placed the stars in the heavens." Patrick went on to tell of God's son - Jesus. The two sisters, being of one heart cried out and said, "Our only desire is to see Him face to face." Patrick baptized both women and they loved Christ with all their hearts - for they had sought the true God for a long time.

THE TWO DRUIDS

Shortly after, both sisters died. Two druids, Mael and Caplait, entered into a great conflict with Patrick over this as the youngest daughter was the foster-daughter of Caplait. Patrick preached the gospel to Caplait and he became a believer to the great anger of the other druid, Mael. "I will win him back to our gods and cause him to leave you," he said to Patrick. Patrick with great patience preached and reasoned with him until he also gave his heart to God. Patrick continued to travel and preach to every town and village with many miracles and signs and wonders.

PATRICK'S PRAYERS FOR IRELAND

Patrick went to a high mountain in the range of Mayo in order to seek God and to fast and pray. For forty days he fasted with watching and prayers and travail. Toward the end of the fast, the mountain was surrounded by many demons in the form of large black birds, screaming and giving off a foul smell. Patrick continued singing psalms and hymns to no avail. Finally Patrick threw his bell at the birds and commanded them to leave. They left and immediately he was surrounded by an angelic choir. Also the angel who was always Patrick's companion, Victor, came and said, "Everything you select shall be yours; every land - both hills and valleys, glens and woods. Every petition shall be granted."

Patrick's first petition was that every Irish man, woman and child would have opportunity to hear the Gospel and secondly, that barbarian invaders should not prevail against the Irish people. Victor commanded Patrick to get down from the mountain but Patrick refused until every petition he asked was granted. Patrick continued to ask for many blessings for Ireland.

PATRICK'S INVITATION

Many of the Celtic saints, because of their close relationship to God, knew when they were going to die and would make arrangement to go to the place which God told them was for their resurrection. In Patrick's case he felt that he should die in Armagh, a place he was deeply attached to. He started to make arrangements to get there but the angel, Victor, forbade him saying, "It is not there that your resurrection is granted to you, go back to the place from which you came, namely Dichu's Barn. But God has granted that your name shall be known and your teaching shall be in Armagh, as if you were still alive in it." So it has been since that time.

PATRICK'S DEPARTING

Patrick returned to Saul, to Dichu's Barn, on Strangford Lough, where he had made his first celebration in Ireland. He gave thanks to God, received Holy Communion from Bishop Tassach and then prayed with the brethren and gave up his spirit to God. *The Tripartite Life* sums up Patrick's life in the following words:

"Now after founding churches in plenty; after consecrating monasteries and baptizing the people of Ireland; after great patience and labor; after destroying idols, and rebuking kings who did not do the will of God; after ordaining three hundred and seventy Bishops and three thousand priests, ministers and laymen; after fasting and prayer; after mercy and clemency; after love of God and his neighbor, he gave up his spirit to God."

It is said that for the twelve nights of his funeral rights, an angelic radiance was seen around his body.

Before he died, on 17th march, 471 A.D. Patrick made this confession:

"If I ever accomplished anything good for the sake of my God, Whom I love, I ask Him to grant that I can shed my

blood with the strangers and captives for His Name's sake. If I, Patrick the sinner, have done any small thing according to the will of God, I attribute it to the gift of God alone. And this is my confession before I die."

COMGALL, ABBOT OF BANGOR, COUNTY DOWN
A.D. 516 (approx.) - A.D. 601

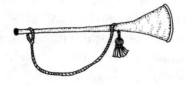

THE PROPHECY

In Jocelyn's, *St. Patrick's Life*, it is stated that Patrick prophesied of Comgall's birth and the foundation of his Abbey at Bangor, sixty years before his appearance in this world[1]. On the day before Comgall's birth, Macniseus, Bishop of Conner, had a vision concerning him. He heard the noise of a chariot outside and announced, "This chariot carries a king." His assistants immediately went outside to check on the chariot. They soon returned saying that the chariot only contained a man named Sedna and his wife, Briga. The Bishop replied, "My children, do not think I have spoken falsely to you for that women, Briga, bears a king, who shall be born tomorrow at sunrise. He will be adorned with all virtues and the world will be illuminated with the luster of his miracles. Not only will many thousands obey him, but a great multitude of princes."

Around the place of his birth a light was seen through the night. He was born in the northern part of Ulster in a region known as Dalaradia.

Being an only son, Comgall was much loved by his parents. He was brought for baptism to a minister, Fedelmid, who had become blind through an accident. Angels were seen at the service. When the minister washed his face in the water in which Comgall was baptized his sight was restored.

THE PILLAR OF FIRE

Comgall grew in wisdom and love of the Lord. One day as he fell asleep in a field his mother approached. As she drew closer, she saw a pillar of fire above his head and became alarmed. When he awoke, Comgall said to her, "Fear not, mother, for I am in no way injured by the celestial fire - but take care not to tell anyone of this."

Comgall later on decided to leave the world and his father's farm in order to dedicate himself to God. His first religious teacher was not too spiritual and one night while he took himself to a place of sin, and so Comgall prayed all night. The following morning he went to meet his teacher in a purposely soiled garment. When the teacher reproved him, he replied, "What is more dangerous Master, to have our outer garment soiled, or our soul? The defilement of your soul last night is much worse than the condition of my garment." Although it silenced his teacher, Comgall's reproof did not stop the vices of his master. Comgall resolved to find a more spiritual place and went to the celebrated monastery of Clonenagh.

Comgall was at least 32 years old when he became a disciple of Fintan, who in turn had been a disciple of the famous Columba of Iona. Eventually Fintan sent him out to start cells in his own part of the country. He went to visit Kieran of Clonmacnoise and preached the gospel everywhere with many signs and wonders. He eventually found an island, Lough Erne, where he led a very austere life. Other younger men submitted themselves to his discipleship but so great were the austerities that seven of them died. Lugidus, through whom he had been ordained, persuaded him to leave the island and continue the work for which he had been destined, founding many churches and cells and preaching the gospel to the lost.

BANGOR MONASTERY

When Comgall came to the place where the river Beg falls into the Belfast Lough, he loved it so much that he founded his famous Monastery of Bangor there. The locality was in the region of Ards - in the province of Ulster. In a short time so many monks flocked to his monastery that there was no room and they were forced to build other houses, not only there but in other places in Ireland. Bangor monastery was the biggest and most famous and in time a whole city was built around its wisdom and sanctity. Apart from the great teaching and discipleship, Bangor Monastery was known for its famous choir.[2]

Many miracles occurred in the monastery as people came to be healed and set free. One day a leper came to the monastery and came across Comgall kneeling with his hands upturned to heaven. As he watched him, he was healed immediately.

THE BRIGHT FLAME

Another time a young monk, Meldan, approached Comgall's cell and as he came near he saw a bright flame which burst forth from the window. He did not dare to go nearer and the following day Comgall sent for him and told him not to reveal what he had seen while he (Comgall), was alive.

THE MONK WHO ROSE FROM THE DEAD

Another time one of the monks was sent from Bangor to another monastery and while there he died. Comgall ordered his body be conveyed back to Bangor. When it arrived, Comgall prayed for him and he was restored to life. The brother told the other monks what had happened after his departure from this life. "I was brought toward heaven by two angels sent by God, and while on our way other angels came to meet us saying, 'Bear this soul back to his body for Comgall, God's servant, has requested it. Therefore bear it to Comgall, with whom the monk will live to an old age."

THE THIEVES

Some thieves came and took fruit and vegetables from the garden time and again. Eventually Comgall went to the garden and prayed, "Oh Omnipotent Lord, who is able to do all things, take away the sight of these robbers until they have confessed their guilt." That night when the robbers entered the enclosure they became blind and were unable to find the exit. At last moved to repent of their crime they called for help and returned the things they had stolen. Their sight was restored and they embraced Christ as their savior and stayed as disciples of Comgall.

Comgall is described in the *Martyrology of Donegal* (See Dr. Todd and Reeves edition pp.122, 123) as, "A man full of God's grace and love who fostered and educated very many other great saints, as he kindled and lit up an unquenchable fire of God's love in their hearts and minds."

COMGALL AND CRITAN

An old man, an Anchorite, named Critan, once visited Comgall during the Easter festival. During the Easter service

Critan saw a bright vision of angels. They touched the hands and mouth and the head of Comgall and joined in his benediction. Critan was very thirsty from fasting, and wanted in his heart to drink from the same cup as Comgall. Although nothing was said, the prophetic gift in Comgall was stirred and he knew the desire of Critan. After the service Comgall entered his cell and took some wine. He then called a servant named Segenus and sent him with the wine to Critan saying, "Bear this wine to the holy man, Critan, who is now very thirsty, and let him drink from my cup, with thanks to God. Tell him from me, "You are a patient and faithful man."

Because of the great influence Comgall had, he is regarded as one of the principal Fathers of the Irish church. Comgall is named among the chief framers of the monastic rules along with, Brigid, Brendan, Patrick, Keiran, Columba, Molassius and Adamnan.

COMGALL AND THE MICE

One time, when the monastery was short of corn, Comgall asked a neighbor, Croidhe, if he would exchange some corn for a silver cup. The man, who was a tyrant, refused, saying, "I would rather the mice eat the corn than you." Comgall replied, "Be it as you say, for the mice will eat your corn and you will not profit." Mice came and ate two heaps of corn which belonged to the avaricious man.

THE DEAD MONK RAISED

On another occasion one of the monks was taken ill and moved to another monastery nearer his family. There he died and his body was brought back to Bangor for burial. Approaching the bier, Abbot Comgall prayed over him and the dead man was instantly restored to life. He later said that he had seen a ladder ascending up into heaven with others going before him. As he began to ascend the ladder, he heard a voice saying that Comgall would not suffer him to ascend the ladder. He lived for another 15 years

THE DEAD YOUNG BOY RAISED

One day after a journey, Comgall returned to his monastery and found that a young boy had died during his absence. He said, "It is my fault that this boy has died before his allotted time." Approaching the body he prayed and the boy was instantly restored to life. He asked the boy, "Do you desire, my son, to remain in this life?" The boy declared that he would rather go to be with the Lord in heaven, and Comgall imparted a blessing, and the boy peacefully yielded his spirit back to God.

A prince who was a great sinner came to the gates of the monastery with an offering of silver, but Comgall sent it back to him with a message saying, "Why do you wish to discharge your iniquities upon us? Bear your own crimes and fruits."

THE BRETHREN FROM IONA

A company of brethren, led by Columba, came by boat from Iona to visit Comgall and during the crossing one of them died. When they arrived at the mouth of the river, Iniver

Beg, they were greeted with much joy. The one that had died they left covered in the boat and went to the monastery. Comgall washed their feet and asked if there was anyone else left on the boat. Columba replied there was one and Comgall requested that he be sent for, so that he also could enjoy the refreshing. Columba said that the brother would not be able to come unless Comgall went to him. Without delay Comgall went to the boat and there he found the dead monk. He was astonished, but took to prayer. "In the Name of Jesus Christ arise and hasten with me to your brothers." The brother awoke and accompanied Comgall to the monastery. Then Comgall noticed that he had lost his sight in one eye. Comgall declared that a monk should not labor under such a defect and he bathed the man's eye. His sight was restored and he could see extremely well all the days of his life.

THE COOK

While Comgall and Columba were sitting at a table taking refreshments, they noticed that the seat belonging to the cook was occupied by a demon. The two abbots were suspicious of the cook and sent for him. When the cook saw the demon sitting in his chair he cried out and rebuked him, "I have not served you since I was young, fly to the desert places where you can hurt no one." The demon fled and Columba and Comgall repented for their suspicions.

COMGALL'S BATH

A certain young man, Aedian by name, the grandson of Dunlainge, after reading the minor prophets with the teacher, Finell, saw in a dream his garments wrapped around a leper. After rising from his sleep he found that his own body was struck with leprosy. He hurried to Comgall and when he reached him he found he had just taken a bath. Comgall instructed him to bathe in the same bath-water and when he stepped out of the bath he was totally cleansed from the leprosy. Aedian returned joyfully and full of praises.

COMGALL'S DEATH

As the end of his life approached Comgall became deaf and suffered a lot of pain. Many believe that it was because of the extremely vigorous austerity that he placed upon himself and the other monks that his body was in such bad condition.

The monks urged him to partake of the Lord's supper, but he refused, saying, "I will receive the Holy Communion from no one else except St. Fiachra. He is the Abbot of Leinster province, who will be sent to me by God."

The angel of the Lord visited Fiachra whose monastery was in Airard and was situated on the banks of the River Barrow. He commissioned Fiachra to go to Comgall and minister to him the Lord's Supper. Upon his arrival he served Communion to Comgall, now in his 85th year. (see Sir James Ware, *De Scriptoribus Hiberniae, lib.i. cap ii. P.14*)

Then Fiachra asked for some keepsakes from Comgall for posterity. The monks agreed, and after praying, Comgall yielded up his spirit to God, his Lord and Creator, in the presence of many godly men. His death occurred 6th May, A.D. 601.

Notes:

[1] The prophecy of Patrick concerning the famous monastery at Bangor.

[2] One day Patrick and his disciples came upon a valley in County Down where they saw the whole valley filled with light and heard heavenly choirs singing praise to God. They called it Vallis Angelorum - The Valley of Angels. [*] This altar became the same place where the monastery at Bangor was established, and the famous "High Choir" which celebrated praise and worship to God like the world had never seen. Historians say that this choir sang continuous praises in relays for 150 years. There were 3,000 monks at Bangor Monastery

In the Ambrosian Library in Milan there is a manuscript preserved which contains some of the Liturgy. The Perennial Praise or Laura Penernnis was founded upon the temple worship in Jerusalem, and they used the same scriptural basis. They were very much like the early Essenes and Therepeutae who sang in a similar fashion in Palestine and Egypt

These early monasteries were more like our present-day Bible schools with many hundreds of students who learned true devotion to Christ and the service of man. They were very evangelistic and the gospel they preached to the heathen was demonstrated with the power of God in many miracles and wonders. They often confronted the druids and many times put to shame the druidic powers by the manifestation of the power of their God.

KIERAN, FIRST BISHOP OF SAIGER, KING'S COUNTY
A D. 352 - A.D. 540

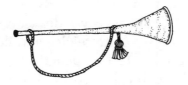

THE LIGHT OF THE GOSPEL

It was said of the early Irish, "Traditions and ties of race and family have weight with the unconverted. They perform superstitious practices, frequent temples, and on certain days have absurd rites and ceremonies. Their parents were superstitious, their friends and neighbors likewise. With difficulty they break the chains which bind them to these things. For a long time our ancestors were sitting in darkness and in the shadow of death, until the people became the Lord's portion and His inheritance. Yet Christianity was known in parts of Ireland during the years preceding the arrival of Patrick. After Ireland's early reign of druidism and heathendom, the land that was desolate was to be made glad. The wilderness was to rejoice and flourish like a lily; the eyes of the blind to be opened; the ears of the deaf unstopped: water to break out over the deserts, and streams in the wilderness. The dry land was to become a pool, and the thirsty land have springs of water. The redeemed of the Lord were to come to Zion with great praise, and everlasting joy was to be upon their heads, they obtained gladness and joy and sorrow and mourning fled away. The light of the Gospel arose over Ireland."

There can be little doubt that from a community at Saigher the first preachers of Christ went forth. In this place was erected one of the first churches in Ireland. A date anterior to the advent of St. Patrick was assigned for the founding of a cell by Kieran (or Ciarain) son of Lughaidh, at Saigher.

In a sermon preached by Rev. N. Murphy in A.D. 1877, Rev Murphy added the following translation of an Irish stanza,

"Kieran, the faithful, noble coharb,
The senior of heaven-loving saints of Erin,
Illustrious, the festival of the royal one,
Whose peaceful Cathedra is great Saigher."

There are many manuscripts on the Life of Kieran - *Life of St. Keiran of Saigher* in Irish transcribed by Brother Michael O'Clery. Among Messrs. Hodges and Smith's collection of Irish Manuscripts in the Royal Irish Academy, are a *Life of St. Kieran of Saigher*. In Marsh's Library, Dublin in the manuscript called, *"Codex Kilkenniessis,"* there is a *Life of St. Kieranus* (Ossoriensis). There is a parchment manuscript belonging to Trinity College, Dublin. Another *Life of Kieran* is in Bodleian Library at Oxford and it is a vellum folio of the 14th century. Colgan furnishes two *Lives of Kieran*. Colgan the writer of the longer *"Life"* must have been a monk living under Kieran's rule. There are many other manuscripts in various libraries around the world.

THE BIRTH OF KIERAN

Kieran was the son of Lughaida, son to Rumond, son of Conall. His mother was Lidania and was the daughter of Manius Kerr, son to Aenguss of Lugad's race. Kieran was the brother of St. Nem Mac Ua Birn, who succeeded St. Enda as Abbot of Aran.

Kieran was born in A.D. 352 at a time when paganism universally prevailed in Ireland. He was born on the island of Clear which is the southernmost land in Ireland. Before his conception, Lidania had a vision in her sleep of a star falling into her mouth. When she related this vision to the Magi (druids) they told her that she would bring forth a son whose virtue and fame would be diffused throughout all Ireland and to the end of time. Growing up, he appeared to have a sweetness of spirit and a well-regulated mind. He was full of wise counsel.

THE KITE

As a youth, Kieran was sitting one day outside and a kite (a large bird), suddenly pounced on a small bird and carried it off. Seeing this, the child grieved much over the fate of the small bird and he prayed for its preservation. The kite flew back and returned the bird, which was then restored to its nest. Although seemingly a small incident, the Lord answered the request of one who was humble and compassionate.

ROME

Kieran continued to his 13th birthday still unconverted. But he did receive some account of the Christian religion. He resolved to go to Rome to find out what he could about the religion. It seems that there in A.D. 382 he became born again. He remained in Rome for 15-20 years learning and collecting copies of the scriptures. He was ordained a priest and returned to Ireland, but on the way he met Patrick in Italy, according to the *Tripartite Life*. Patrick prophesied to Kieran, "Proceed to Ireland before me, and go to a fountain in the middle of Ireland which is called Fuaran, on the northern and southern line of division in the island; build a monastery on that spot, for there you will be held in honor, and it shall be at the place of your resurrection." To this Keiran replied, "The place where that fountain springs I do not know." Then Patrick answered, "My dearly-beloved brother, proceed with full confidence and the Lord will be your guide; receive this bell which shall be the companion of your journey and will not sound until you come to the fountain I have spoken of. When you arrive there the bell will ring out clearly and sound sweetly. After thirty years, I will meet you in that place." With the kiss of peace these great men of God departed to their respective destinations.

KILKENNY

Kieran arrived in the present Kilkenny city and there he collected his first band of disciples and established his first Irish monastery. He sang Psalms and hymns, practiced his Christianity and confronted the druids and their pagan followers.

According to his *Life*, after his arrival in Ireland, Kieran made his way, by the Lord's leading, to the fountain of Fuaran. This is generally thought to have been identified as a stream which passes near the present Seirkyran, or Kieran, which was formerly know as Saigher. It is a small village presently situated in the Barony of Ballybritt, Kings County, not far from the Slieve Bloom mountains. Kieran's bell rang when he arrived at that fountain according to Patrick's prophesy. The bell was said to have been made for St. Germanus, the

Bishop and instructor of St. Patrick. The bell had been called Bodhran-the mute.

THE WILD BOAR

When Keiran came to the place where he decided to build his dwelling, a wild boar fled from him as he sat down under a tree. The boar afterwards came back and became domesticated and helped Kieran build his house. The animal with its tusks helped break down twigs and branches for the walls.

Kieran was known for his spiritual authority over the animals. A fox, a deer, a wolf and a badger came to him and stayed with him. It wasn't long before his disciples found him, and in the place of his wicker hut there grew up a great monastery and subsequently an ecclesiastical city.

Kieran began to attract many people from the surrounding areas to whom he spoke of salvation. Many Ossorians became Christians and were baptized by him.

About the same time, three other prelates ministered in the southern part of Ireland with some success - all before Patrick arrived on the scene These were Ailbe, Ibar and Declan, who labored in the neglected vineyard of the Lord.

THE PIGS AND SHEEP

As the monastery was built many miracles accompanied the ministry. At one time the steward came to Kieran and said that they needed to purchase some swine. Kieran replied that the Lord would send them. The next day a sow and her litter appeared at their gate. A while later the same steward told Kieran that they needed sheep and Kieran told them that the same Lord who sent the swine would send the sheep. The following day there were 27 sheep standing at the gate. After his father's death, Keiran's mother, Liadain, became a Christian and raised up a nunnery at Killyon.

THE DEAD RAISED

One time a rich man named Fintan brought his son's dead body to Kieran, asking that he raise him up. Kieran approached the body of Leoghaire and through the prayer of faith in Christ, he was raised and returned to his father. The young man lived for a long time and in gratitude Fintan gave to the monastery the village of Rathfera (Rath-fearinn).

A son of Erc had maliciously killed a horse belonging to St. Patrick. Being apprehended by the soldiers of Aengus, the man was put in chains ready to be put to death. Upon the request of friends, Kieran procured his ransom at a considerable cost. But after his liberation the gold and silver disappeared. The royal recipient angrily asked Kieran how he dared to impose a phantom treasure on the king. Kieran replied that everything of the earth would return to the earth. Aengus became enraged and uttered threats against Kieran and he immediately fell to the ground, blind. St. Carthage, a disciple and grandson to Aengus begged Kieran to restore the king's sight. Kieran approached the prostrate form and raised him after giving a sharp rebuke. The king afterwards bestowed many gifts upon Kieran and the monastery.

THE HARPISTS

This same King Aengus had certain harpists in his court who sang ballads and played music. While passing through the territory of Muscra Thire, in the province of Munster, they were murdered and their bodies were thrown into a lake, and their harps were suspended on a tree on the borders of the Lough. Aengus, not knowing what happened to his musicians, remembered that Kieran was gifted with prophecy, and not willing to consult the druids because he had become a Christian, he came to Kieran and learned from him what had happened to his harpists. When the king had discovered the fate of the harpists, he asked Kieran to accompany him to the lake. After they had fasted all day the water drew back and revealed the bodies of the harpers. In the Name of Christ, Kieran commanded them to arise, and, seeming to awake after a sleep, they took their harps down from the tree and began to play sweet music for the king and for Kieran, and a crowd of people who were gathered there. The lake was afterwards named, Loch na Cruitireadh, "Lake of the Harpers," although the water in the lake had dried up.

THE SOLDIERS

On another occasion the Chief of Aengus with his retainers, while passing through Ossory, saw some swine belonging to St. Etchean and ordered his soldiers to kill one of them. While they were preparing to roast it, their enemies surprised them and killed the chief and some of the soldiers on the banks of a rivulet called Brosnach.

An account of this disaster was brought to Kieran by his disciple, Carthage, who asked Keiran if he could have the bodies removed so that they would not be devoured by wild beasts. When Kieran came to the place, the cart was not big enough to remove the bodies. He then cried out with a loud voice that in the Name of Christ all those who were killed should arise and follow him. All of the soldiers who were resurrected that day became monks under St. Kieran.

One time when Patrick, The King of Munster, and 20 chiefs with their attendants, were guests of Kieran. He ordered eight oxen to be prepared for their entertainment. When they realized that this would not be sufficient for all the guests plus the monks themselves, Kieran said that the Lord fed thousands with a few loaves and fishes they should be content with what they had and trust God. The food lasted as long as it was needed and when he blessed a fountain, wine of good quality was found.

KIERAN, THE QUEEN, AND THE BLACKBERRY BUSH

One day Kieran felt led to spread a cloth over some blackberry bushes to preserve the blackberries through the cold weather, to keep them for an occasion which he had some foreknowledge about.

After Easter, King Aengus and his wife, Queen Ethnea Huathach, came to the castle of Conchryd, Chieftain of Ossary. The visiting king and queen had been entertained with a great banquet by Conchryd, who was a man of great personal attraction. Unfortunately, the queen conceived an unlawful passion for him which was accompanied by a dishonorable proposal on her part. Being a man of virtue, Conchryd rejected her advances, and the queen feigned sudden illness in order to remain behind in his castle after her husband's departure.

Being asked what might help her get well again she said would be made better by blackberries. She supposed that as the season had passed no one would be able to find any blackberries. The chief went to Kieran with the account of the circumstances. He expressed apprehension at the queen remaining behind after the king's departure. Kieran went to get the blackberries from his bush in the woods and sent them to the queen. Upon eating them Ethnea found her passion for Conchryd cease. She prostrated herself at the feet of Kieran, confessing her sin and asking for forgiveness. Kieran replied with a sigh, "Oh Queen, I cannot release you from an impeding death, for daughter, your enemies shall kill both you and our sovereign the king, on the same day."

This word was fulfilled in A.D. 489 when Aengus and the queen were killed on the same day at the battle of Cell Osnadha, now Kelliston in the country of Carlow. This battle was fought against them by Muircheartach Mac Erca, by Illann and Ailill, sons of Dunlaing, and by Eochaidh Guineach. These events are rendered very notorious, through the accounts left in our ancient annals (See Colgan's *Acta Sanctorium Hiberniae, Martil v, First Life, chapter xix. Second Life, lect vii. Officium pp.460 -468*).

RAISED FROM THE DEAD

A woman named Eathylla fell, and had such severe fractures that she soon died. The third day Kieran prayed and her life was restored. Another friend of Kieran's, Cronan, was killed by a Munster officer. When Kieran found this out, he went and raised Cronan from the dead after seven days.

THE KING STRUCK DUMB

One day King Ailill, the king of Munster, spoke reproachful words in the presence of Kieran and he was deprived of his speech for seven days. Then he asked for forgiveness of Kieran who then blessed his tongue and his speech was restored.

That very ancient and interesting place commonly called St. Kyran's is reputed to have been the seat of the oldest bishopric in Ireland. While Kieran lived there Saints Carthage and Bathene were disciples under him. He was also visited by St.Medran and St.Odhran who were brothers. Another St. Kieran who was the Abbot of Clonmacnoise, a fellow disciple under Finian, Abbot of Clonard and St. Brendan of Birr and Brendan of Clonfert also visited him.

MINISTRY

Kieran visited and ministered in Cornwall, England, where there are many memorials.

Kieran converted many from paganism. He ordained a great number of bishops and clergy, and had numerous angelic visitations. On one occasion he asked God for the production of a fountain in a certain place shown him by an angel. Soon after his prayer was granted, and many sick people were healed at this spring, which was called, "The Well of Kieran."

In the language of an ancient Irish writer, "His heart was chaste and shining, and his mind like the foam of the waves, or the color of the swan in the sunshine; without sin finding a resting place in his heart," (*Irish Lives*-O'Hannlon).

Before his death, while engaged in prayer, the angel of God appeared to him. At this time he was bowed down with old age and he asked these favors of the Almighty through the celestial messenger. He asked that all who celebrated the festival of his death should have prosperity in this life and be happy in the next, and that the people of Ossory should have victory over their enemies, if they themselves did not invade the territory of others.

In one of the *Lives* in Colgan's possession it is recounted that as his death approached, he called his monks together and said to them, "The Lord now summons me to Himself, and I am solicitous about you; wherefore I commend you to the care of God, and to my son, Carthage." With this he released his spirit happily. It is said that 30 of his bishops that same day departed and went with him to the heavenly country. This was a manifestation of his, and their desire which had already been granted by the Lord. As Patrick prophesied, this was the place of his resurrection in about A.D. 540. He was well over 100 years old.